Dodging Bullets

by

David Wittlinger

Cover photos and design by the author

Introduction

"Untainted by Technology" was an actual advertising slogan of Royal Enfield in the 1990s. I coined my own catch phrase, "A 500cc motorcycle with the performance of 250cc!", as a tongue-in-cheek admiration for a classic machine built for a slower pace of life.

I love old machinery. I can stand in awe in front of a running hit-n-miss engine at an old farm equipment display. I can appreciate the experimentation that was a huge part of engineering back in the infancy of the internal combustion engine and the vehicles it propelled.

I'm a self-taught mechanic in the strictest sense. My father grew up on a farm where equipment was repaired on-site not because of convenience but as a necessary exercise in frugality. He too was mostly self-taught about engines and machines but he didn't possess the natural knack for it that I came to have. By the time I was in my twenties I had eclipsed his level of skill, knowledge and number of tools.

There is, however, a level of comfort to my knowledge. Modern vehicles frequently perplex me thanks to the myriad of electronic sensors and controls. The engine bays are crammed with 'stuff' that make repairs difficult and the driving experience is hindered by various driver aids. Though arguably more reliable than vehicles decades older I no longer get excited about new models or technology. They have surpassed my comfort level and interest in working on them. While I used to be a proficient wrench-turner in the evenings and on weekends I've increasingly found myself seeking other pursuits. My tools go mostly unused and my garage has become a place to store cars instead of work on them.

Not quite a decade ago I developed an interest in motorcycles. Though my father had a few when I was growing up my focus had always been on four wheeled devices. I found in motorcycles some of what had been disappearing from my cars: the tactile feel of speed and a mechanical simplicity I didn't think still existed.

So more of that would be better, right? If my literary idol Peter Egan could find happiness repairing decrepit old motorcycles why couldn't I?

This book is the story of my foray into a familiar world (mechanics) but on machinery I only had a rudimentary knowledge of (motorcycles). As I mentioned I am not a professional mechanic; I've had no training and have learned a great deal over the years by doing it wrong a time or two first. The following is not meant to be an instruction manual or recommendation of repair methods.

The Project

Be careful what you wish for.

I was desperate for a hobby vehicle to tinker with. My job is mostly typing on keyboards and pushing paper around. My fingers yearned to spin nuts onto bolts. I couldn't recall the last time I'd banged my head on the underside of a hood or gotten a piece of rust in my eye. I missed the mental challenge of working out in my head how something would come apart or go back together. I was frankly bored.

Though the stalls of my garage were full with four-wheeled vehicles there remained enough room to house and work on a motorcycle. I already owned two modern bikes; both were Triumphs that provided reliable service and required little maintenance. I liked the simplicity and ease of repair access that motorcycles offered and decided that an old bike should be my next mechanical challenge. Besides, I hadn't used my vast catalog of swear word combinations in quite some time.

I began browsing the internet with more frequency(I admit I'm always at the ready for something interesting), scanning advertisements on Craigslist and Facebook Marketplace looking for a likely candidate. The obvious choice was a vintage Triumph twin but I felt it would be too similar to the modern Bonneville I already owned. Norton Commandos called to me but the buy-in wasn't cheap and several would-be 'experts' kept talking me out of them. I wasn't wild about BSAs. The Japanese brands have never kept my interest despite their competent engineering and reliability. I browsed Urals and Moto Guzzis but the exotic nature and questionable parts availability held me at bay. I'd never cared for two stroke engines which eliminated several other choices. I wanted something simple, perhaps with a single cylinder. The Triumph Tiger Cub seemed to fit the bill but I couldn't seem to locate one.

When I had shopped for my first modern 'retro' bike the two I considered were the Triumph that I eventually bought and the Royal Enfield Bullet. The Bullet Classic 500 had a fabulous vintage look and an affordable price but the lack of local dealerships and somewhat lackluster performance had steered me to a used Triumph Bonneville. The Triumph had been the right decision but I still gazed wistfully at Bullets on the rare occasion I saw one. After speaking with a few owners and reading everything I could find I added the older 'iron barrel' model to my short list of candidates. If I was going to go 'old school' then I wanted the authentic experience. Though they weren't really 'old' machines they retained the appearance and technology of something built many decades before. The more I researched them the more I was convinced a Bullet would be the right project to undertake and with a couple grand in my 'play money' account I placed my wish.

A Brief History Lesson

The Royal Enfield company of Redditch, England dates all the way back to 1851. Their initial product was sewing needles but this was followed by bicycle parts and then complete bicycles. With the growing popularity of gasoline engines motorcycles logically followed and even cars for a brief period. The company also manufactured parts for firearms; the legend 'Built Like A Gun, Goes Like A Bullet' would grace Royal Enfield's advertising for decades.

Ultimately, Royal Enfield would concentrate on motorcycles. The first model designated 'Bullet' appeared in 1931. It was updated in 1949 and again in 1955. The 1955 Bullet is the bike we still recognize today, though it has gone through some major changes while retaining the essential appearance and specifications.

Royal Enfield of England disappeared after 1970, another casualty of the endless mergers and poor management of all British motorcycle brands in the late 1960s. The brand could have easily joined the other nearly forgotten names like Matchless, Velocette, BSA and AJS but for a fortunate military contract with the Indian government way back in 1949.

India at the time was part of the British Empire, which meant British companies got preferential treatment when it came to government contracts. The Indian Army selected the Royal Enfield Bullet as their border patrol machine of choice. Originally supplied as 'kits' in a box, Bullets were soon built in a new factory in Madras. In 2013 a new modern factory was built in Chennai to bring Royal Enfield into the modern age. By this time the classic look had been augmented by a new 'unit construction' engine (meaning the transmission case was cast as part of the engine case), electronic ignition, fuel injection and disc brakes. The machine remains intensely popular in India and is something of a status symbol and national pride.

The 'original' Bullet with it's cast iron cylinder barrel, points ignition and drum brakes I regarded as a more 'pure' motorcycle. Though the newer models are more reliable, safer and less prone to oil leaks the idea of being able to ride an authentic 1955 motorcycle that wasn't actually sixty years old was appealing. The Bullet was the oldest motorcycle in continuous production and had been made in the millions. Although scarce in the U.S. every corner garage in India had parts and someone who could fix them. I imagined owning and repairing a Bullet would be as much of an experience as riding one.

The Hunt

Despite the popularity of 'retro' styled motorcycles the Bullet remained an obscure oddity in the United States. A few had trickled in over the years before a concerted effort from an independent importer, Classic Motorworks, made them more accessible. Dealers remained few and far between and many did not sell motorcycles as their primary business. Royal Enfield was frequently offered alongside Chinese scooters and other inexpensive machines. Though some dealers were enthusiastic many were just hoping to add to their bottom line. The decades old design, lower build quality from India (sorry; it's true) and inexperienced dealership mechanics didn't help the brand's reputation. The Bullet was a fine machine by 1960s standards but the cheap chrome, flimsy switches and weak metallurgy didn't play well in more modern times despite it's low price. Royal Enfield of India would eventually buy out the private importer and begin setting up their own distribution in the 2010 decade in anticipation of selling new additional models, the Himalayan and a new retro style twin cylinder 650 machine. Neither of these bikes share anything of note with the Bullet which remained in production and was still sold alongside the modern bikes.

All of this meant that finding an 'iron barrel' Bullet in the USA would be more difficult than getting a later unit construction, or 'UCE', model. I didn't just want another motorcycle; I wanted a project of some sort to tinker with or possibly rebuild.

At last one did show up that met my criteria: iron barrel engine, a color I didn't hate (blue), not running and an asking price of $2600--which was what a running one would fetch. I didn't inquire about it as the price was simply too high for one the ad stated, "Not running, only needs $80 worth of parts to fix". If that were true the owner should fix it himself! As a buyer I couldn't determine if the engine was repairable or if the transmission had all the gears or if the electrical system worked. It was simply too risky.

A week or so later the ad moved to the top of the feed again with a new price of $2200. Now we were getting closer to reality. After some hesitation I contacted the seller only to be informed that a buyer was to come that weekend and make the purchase. I thanked her for the reply and flippantly offered that if the deal fell through she should let me know.

The weekend came and went and I was surprised when I received a message that the bike had not sold as the alleged buyer never showed up. At this point I asked more questions about the bike and found out it had been off the road for a couple of years. A valve had dropped and been broken off by the piston. The head was off the bike and it allegedly just needed a new valve and seat to return it to operating condition. Hmm. I still wouldn't know if the rest of the bike was intact or functional. It stood to reason it probably was fine; the valve breakage would have been a sudden catastrophic failure on a running machine. Still, I was worried that the repairs may quickly surpass the price of a Bullet in good running condition. The tightwad in me couldn't bear the idea of being upside-down in a motorcycle I wasn't even sure I'd even like when I finally rode it.

I politely expressed my concerns to the woman and advised it was too much of a risk for me at the asking price. She countered with "make us an offer". I scratched my chin in contemplation as I read this latest response. What *was* it worth to me? She seemed eager to sell and tearing into an engine was an appealing project despite the potential cost. I told her I'd think about it and would let her know in a day or so. I priced parts on the internet, figured out the distance to pick it up (it was a couple hours' drive), what I could get parting it out if it wound up being hopeless, considered my spouse's likely eye-roll at yet another hopeless machine taking up space in the garage and decided it was worth $1500 for me to take a risk on it. I logged on to my computer to send this insulting offer and found another message from the would-be seller.

"If you come get it this weekend you can have it for $1200".

The Purchase

As I drove down to Maryland from my home in Pennsylvania I reviewed the information I'd gleaned from the subsequent phone call with the seller. Her husband had purchased the Bullet from her brother, a fellow who apparently would buy and fix up motorcycles to 'flip' for profit. The bike hailed from the Chicago area which is where the sellers had previously lived and they'd brought the bike with them when they moved to rural northern Maryland. The husband had bought the bike with the same intent I currently had of repairing it, meaning it was already broken when he obtained it. A 2007 model showing 8300 miles on the odometer it had been off the road for three years.

I arrived at the residence and met with the husband, a guy in his 30s who led me to an outdoor shed/workshop. The Bullet was inside, parked next to an equally neglected Buell sport bike. The fuel tank was off and the cylinder head was missing from the barrel which was covered with a plastic bag. The carburetor and decompression valve were zip tied to the spine of the frame. The seller showed me a box of parts containing the head, broken valve, valve parts, head bolts and other pieces of hardware I'd have to figure out where they went. The fuel tank appeared undamaged. The medium blue paint had a nice aged patina while the chrome on the fenders and tank looked better than I'd expected. Indian Enfield chrome was not known for it's resistance to rust and I had expected to find flecks of brown on everything. The only part that looked truly bad was the exhaust outlet pipe; it had quite a bit of rust on it and I knew it would never clean up well. As I took stock I noted the original seat was missing along with the muffler. The bike had been fitted with low cafe' style handlebars but the original ones were included. The seat had been replaced with a 'bobber' style solo seat that looked entirely too small and woefully uncomfortable. Another seat was in a box with some of the parts and I assumed it would be the optional 'solo' seat that was offered by Royal Enfield suppliers. The tires were holding air and the brakes, engine and transmission were all 'free' and unstuck. The bike was the exact type of project I was looking for; it had 'good bones' and most of the work needed I felt was within my skill level.

It turned out the sellers were desperate for money which is why the price had plummeted so quickly. Though they did not share their financial woes with me I surmised that an impending bill (mortgage?) was looming and the sale of the non-functional Bullet was a quick solution. The seller seemed remorseful at letting it go but nonetheless took my offered cash. The title was presented and I confirmed the VIN matched the bike. It was in a woman's name with a Chicago address and I assumed it was his wife. In fact it was not; the name on the title was that of the owner that had sold it to the brother-in-law...essentially two owners ago! The upside was that the title had been signed by the person on the title and one quirk of Pennsylvania was you only needed the signature to bring in a vehicle from out of state. I didn't anticipate it being a problem though I did cringe a little inside. There was still the possibility the bike could become a paperweight if I couldn't get clear ownership.

The shed was at the top of a fairly steep driveway that I couldn't back my truck and trailer up to. I checked the brakes, hopped astride the partially disassembled machine and pushed off to coast down the hill. The front brake worked but I could tell it was sticking while the rear provided less than enthusiastic slowing. I made it safely down the incline and strapped the bike to the trailer, thanked the seller and climbed into my truck for the drive home. I'd either purchased a fun way to occupy my time in the coming months or had just taken in an orphan that would wreak misery upon my existence.

Assessment

    With the Bullet home in my garage it was time to assess just what it was that I'd bought. I posted a few photos on some Royal Enfield message boards and soon found out what I'd thought was a 'Sixty-Five' model was actually a Royal Enfield Bullet Deluxe. The Deluxe part alluded to the chrome fuel tank and fenders. The chrome also would have included a battery box (missing) and chain guard (missing). Being near the end of iron barrel production mine was also equipped with the five speed transmission instead of the ancient Albion four speed and an electric starter to supplement the kick start.

    The electric start option generated a great deal of chatter on the internet; none positive. The starter was bolted to the front of the engine and engaged the 'primary' (transmission) drive by means of a 'sprag clutch'. The sprag clutch is similar in operation to a ratchet pulled from your toolbox. It spins freely in one direction while engaging in the opposite. Sort of. Bullets, being from another era, can suffer from 'kick back' when starting. This occurs when the engine fires at the wrong time, spinning the crankshaft backwards instead of forwards. If this happens while kicking the bike over it can hurt your leg. When it happens using the electric start the resulting force blows the sprag clutch apart, showering lots of little metal bits into the primary case. The consensus was that it was not a question of *if* this would happen, only *when*.

The good news was that Bullets are generally very easy to kick start so I decided to pretend mine did not have electric start. I would leave it in place only for 'emergencies'.

I laid out the various spare parts on the floor and tried to figure out where they went. It wasn't terribly difficult and all of the parts for the engine were accounted for but I also noted several items for the bike were missing. There was no air cleaner or battery box. Four non-original turn signals were not attached to the bike and I wasn't sure where the leads were. There was no front brake light switch and only one rear view mirror that was not original. While I had the main exhaust pipe there was no muffler. The seat that was in the box was a duplicate of the ridiculous bobber seat that was on the bike. The chain guard was absent but a small piece of chrome still bolted to the swing arm told the story of it's demise. There was no side stand nor did it appear there ever had been but the bike did have a solid center stand which I deemed acceptable.

I continued to assess the condition of the bike,

something I should have done before I pulled out my wad of cash at the seller's residence. The completely dead battery was a tiny item stuffed into the left side tool box. The right side tool box (actually part of the air inlet system--more on that later) was filled with electrical devices that certainly didn't belong there. The wiring was a mess and had clearly been 'modified' to move items to places they weren't supposed to be. The tail light had been replaced by a vintage Lucas replica piece but the lens was broken.

The cafe' bars, relocated battery, missing muffler and silly seat all indicated the previous owner (hereafter referred to disparagingly as 'PO') had attempted to turn the Bullet into some sort of cafe' racer. This style of bike was popularized by British youth in the 1960s who modified their machines for high speed running during illicit races between roadside cafe's. Dropped handlebars, moving the foot controls to the rear, removing air cleaners and modifying the exhaust system were all part of the package. A proper cafe' racer would be able to 'do the ton' (100mph).

The idea of making a Royal Enfield Bullet into a cafe' racer to me was frankly ludicrous. The 500cc single would quickly shed itself of reciprocating parts if pressed to much more than 70 mph without extensive modifications. Though the PO's goal was probably just to get the appearance of a cafe' bike the execution was...how do I say this diplomatically?...piss-poor.

The first order of business was to rid the bike of the ridiculous handlebars. I'm sorry, but my fifty-four year old spine in no way would tolerate the contortionist riding position the bars demanded. The bike was an ergonomic nightmare with the low bars, rearward sloping seat and standard foot controls. Off came the old bars which were tossed unceremoniously against the far wall. In the process of removing them and installing the originals I found that there are four nuts that clamp them in place. These nuts are shouldered in such away that allow them to seat properly against the clamp. Two of the four were installed upside-down.

This would set the tone for most of the PO's workmanship.

With the original bars properly bolted down I attached the various switch gear for the lights and so forth. There are two plastic housings that contain the switches which are clamped to the bars by tightening screws. I snugged these screws down fully but was puzzled to find the switch assemblies were not actually tight and would spin on the bars with little force. I noted the cafe bars had electrical tape wrapped around them. I measured the diameter of both the original and cafe bars and they were identical. Scratching my head I could only assume the switch housings were distorted in such a way that they would no longer clamp tightly to the bars. The PO solution was to wrap electrical tape around the bars as traction. I tried doing the same thing but found it both ugly and not wholly effective.

Shelving that problem for later I took a look at the seat then set about removing it. I would later regard the fastening method of the seat as the epitome of the ineptitude of the soon-to-be-despised PO. The seat had two springs under it providing for some level of shock absorption which was fairly common on very old motorcycles with rigid rear frames that had no other suspension. The rear of the seat via the springs was attached with some bizarre brackets that somehow required the springs to be removed from the seat, an exercise that defined the word 'fiddly'. This was followed by the forward attachment that had been accomplished via a clasp normally seen as a latch for attaching a padlock to a shed door. I kid you not. With the diabolical seat removed and tossed aside with mild distaste the bike looked very naked.

I began compiling a list of needed parts. In the process I took a closer look at the engine, wanting to make sure the cylinder was not damaged. As I cycled the headless engine and watched the piston bob up and down I noticed that what I thought was a valve relief was a rather jagged chunk of the piston missing.

Shit.

I quickly hopped online and looked up the Worst Case Scenario; the price of a new piston from England was $70. Well, not hateful. I added a piston to the list of gaskets and seals, then checked the head and valve to see which valve it was that had broken. The chamber of the head had not been impacted by the valve that I could see but...wait a minute...

The valve guide looked as if someone had been

at it with a pair of pliers. This by itself wouldn't have been so terrible as the guide is replaceable but the head adjacent to the guide was also missing a chunk. Had the valve caused this damage or the ham-fisted PO? It didn't matter. The head was 'iffy' at this point. Adding the cost of a guide, valve and having to take it to a machine shop to get the guide replaced the cost was not the mere $80 the seller had suggested. An entire head could be more cost effective.

I tabled the cylinder head problem and picked up the gas tank which I'd noticed earlier held some amount of fuel sloshing around inside. I grumbled in irritation as I tried to understand the logic of someone who would unbolt and remove a fuel tank and not drain the fuel out of it when they knew the bike wasn't going to run for some time. I'd looked in the tank when I'd bought the bike and it just looked a little dirty. I grabbed a fuel can and opened the tap. Nothing came out. I moved the lever to the 'reserve' position and was rewarded with a stream of fuel. Using an old shirt as a filter I drained the fuel into the can. Sure enough the shirt showed a bunch of light brown detritus when I was done. The tank would need a severe cleaning to remove rust.

There were more challenges than I expected...which I should have expected. I pushed the 'pause' button on working on the Bullet and decided I should make sure I could get title to the thing before I pumped any money into it. With some creative pencil scratching I obtained a tracing of the frame VIN stamp and set off to the local notary with the title.

Electrons

Pennsylvania does not have a department of motor vehicles like most states. There is a central office that administers all of the documentation for the state but vehicle titles and licensing is handled at the local level by independent notary publics. It's actually a good system because there are offices everywhere and you rarely need to wait in line for service. The notary public has computer interface with the main office in the state capital and most transactions are instantaneous.

Most.

I took my pencil tracing of the VIN and the title to my local notary. As the buyer I need to supply the current odometer reading and the price paid for the vehicle. If my purchase had been between two in-state people both parties would need to be present to confirm identities and other facts. As I was bringing my purchase in from out of state it was actually easier, though it does rely substantially on the honor system. The information was entered into the computer at which point I'd typically receive a fresh new Pennsylvania title.

Typically.

"Hmm," the office worker mused. "It won't accept this VIN."

Uh-oh. I'd never encountered this before and I'd bought quite a few vehicles out of state. I hoped it was simply a matter of it being a weird Indian motorcycle and not something more sinister.

"What does that mean?" I bravely inquired.

"It means it doesn't show in the system. Could be because it's been out of the system for awhile or some other reason. They will have to process it manually."

"How long does that take?"

"Ten days to two weeks," was the response.

Okay, it wasn't the end of the world. The thing didn't run so there was no hurry to get a license plate for it. My main goal was to get a clean title in my name so I didn't have to worry about the Illinois title and the person's name on it that I had never met. I had gone on the internet and used search engines as well as social media. While I was able to find a photo of the address of the PO the name had been far too common to pin down. The unknown female no longer resided at the address on the title.

I left the title with the notary to be hand delivered to the Department of Transportation building in Harrisburg. I need not have worried; within two weeks a title arrived in my name with no further drama. The Royal Enfield and it's VIN would return to worry me again later when I applied for insurance.

While I was waiting for the title I decided to tackle the electrics as they wouldn't cost me anything to try to straighten out. I turned a plastic bucket upside down, sat next to the bike and hooked up my jump start pack to the main connections after removing the hopelessly dead battery.

Turning on the key got me movement from the AMP gauge and a dimly glowing light in the speedometer. I flipped the switch on for the headlight. Nothing. Pulled the sealed beam out of the nacelle and tested it manually. It worked. Sigh...something amiss in the switch or wiring then.

There were no turn signals so no point in toying with that. Squeezing the front brake lever would do nothing for a brake light as the switch was absent. Pressed down on the foot pedal for the rear brake and--predictably--nothing. I also checked for spark from the plug lead and that did work. Pulled the cover off the ignition and checked the point gap which was spot-on and clean. We had fire; all we needed was fuel after the engine was back together.

Back to the brake light. The PO had replaced the cheap looking 1970s style Bullet tail light with a Lucas replica in a nice chrome housing. The wires for the light ran down from the lamp and through a hole in the fender...with no rubber grommet. I removed the rear fender (the wiring is attached to the underside) and found the fender metal had worn through the wiring for the light.

Imagine my lack of surprise. I removed the tail lamp and disassembled it, put heat shrink tubing over the chafed section and sealed it up. When I removed the tail light lens I found it was broken into two pieces; add another part to the list. I poked through my bin of body grommets and found one that fit nicely in the fender. Tested the lamp on my battery pack and it lit up. Now it was just a matter of dealing with the wiring connections that were on the underside of the fender. It was no surprise to find some snipped off wires just hanging from the harness that I suspected (correctly) were for the rear turn signals. I mocked things up, studied a few wiring diagrams from the internet (one of which even exactly matched what I had) and started checking for current. With the key and headlamp switch on I could get a steady light at the tail but still no brake.

The rear brake light switch is located inside the left tool box and is a marvel of engineering. A wire 'hook' connects a spring to the brake lever. The spring is attached to a small rod that slides fore and aft within the electrical switch. When the brake lever is depressed it pulls the hook, spring and rod which slides inside the switch and completes the power circuit to the rear brake light. I removed the switch, cleaned it, found an improper size screw not holding one of the wires in, replaced the screw, put it back in and adjusted the brake lever until the switch triggered power to the rear light. I found the pedal had to be adjusted low and pressed quite hard to make the light come on. Despite there being several holes in a cam to preload the spring none seemed to make it better. Well, it now worked. Sort of.

As I mentioned before the PO had hacked and extended some of the wiring to move the battery into the left tool box and the rectifier and some other components into the right side one. Additionally, the starter button had been redirected from the handlebar to a push button stuck into the forward facing portion of the left tool box. I don't know if this had been done because the original button failed or as some further way-cool cafe' racer thing. I hated the wiring. It was a convoluted mess and I couldn't abide it. I hadn't planned on using the electric start anyway so...

Out came the push button and the entire harness that went to the starter. It was a separate sub-harness so after unbolting it from the starter it was quickly removed. The missing push button left a rough, garish hole in the tool box that I couldn't find a suitable body plug for so reluctantly stuck the inoperative button back in the hole.

After consulting with an internet friend whose father had a similar Bullet I obtained photos of where the other components were supposed to be. The voltage regulator and rectifier were intended to be under the seat in a position where they would get some cooling airflow. Wedged inside the right hand tool box they certainly weren't so I returned them to their proper position. Some added wire length for a fuse holder and main power cable were removed then everything heat shrinked for protection and tidied up.

I wasn't sure what to do about the battery. I preferred to have the toolbox empty for carrying small items (tools?) but I didn't have a proper battery tray. The originals were frankly kind of ugly while taking up space on the left side just forward of the tool compartment. I nearly pulled the trigger on a used setup on Ebay but held off because of the opposite side.

The same area on the right side of the bike held the air inlet box, also missing on mine. The air filter actually was supposed to reside in the 'tool box' with a connecting rubber hose going to the air inlet box which was then connected to the carburetor via another rubber hose. All I had was the tool box and a open carb throat. I'd read that the rubber hoses for the inlet system were short-lived. The whole setup seemed silly and unattractive to me. I decided to add a small air filter onto the mouth of the carb for simplicity and appearance.

Except then you would be staring at the backside of the equally unattractive battery box on the other side.

Ultimately I wound up doing what the PO had done which incensed me to no small degree: I placed a sealed battery inside the left tool box and called it sorted.

Floppy-ness

The following day I decided to check on the rather floppy rear brake lever. The underside of the Bullet was covered in quite a bit of black filth. After laying down a lot of newspaper under the bike I took some parts cleaner and a stiff brush and cleaned things up as best as I could. I found the brake lever on the right side pivots a shaft that runs across the underside of the motorcycle to the left. This was necessary as the original Bullet was a 'standard British' arrangement when it was designed, meaning the shifter was on the right and brake on the left. After standardization of motorcycle controls in the 1970s many export machines such as my Bullet had to be modified to comply. The results were often levers with long throws and shifters with vague feel. The brake lever on a Bullet has to also clear the exhaust pipe which means it decreases the bike's ground clearance on that side as well. Fortunately the five speed gearbox was designed with left foot shifting in mind and actually works quite well.

The brake lever shaft passes through the frame in two places and pivots inside bronze bushings. The bushing on the left side had worked itself loose and the shaft was now rattling around in the frame. I tapped the bushing back into the frame where it belonged and added a zip tie on the shaft that I hoped would keep it in place. The design seemed like it should have a cotter pin through the shaft to keep the bushing from moving but I found nothing on the parts diagram to indicate any thought had been given to it.

In the process of doing this I noticed the chain was also really floppy. Floppy-ness seemed to be a theme with this bike. The internet indicated that with the bike on it's stand there should be about 2" of flop...er...slack. That is still a lot but mine was probably another half inch beyond that. Okay, let's adjust the chain which is thickly crusted with grease and grime. Still waiting for my on-order digital shop manual I pondered the various bolts holding the rear wheel on, loosened the ones that seem to matter and take out the slack. Instead of threaded adjusters like 'real' motorcycles the RE uses stepped 'snail' cams to set the adjustment. These will naturally want to flop loose at the slightest provocation whilst you attempt to tighten things. I marked their current location before loosening, then moved both one spot and attempted to re-tighten...except every time I turned in the axle nut the opposite side would twist backward (loosen). What the...? I pondered this off and on throughout the day as I couldn't get it to stay. More Googling which found much commentary about "don't trust the cams to be equal; measure the alignment". Hmm. I tried using the 'string method' but found working around the center stand to be problematic and ultimately inaccurate. With the cams equal the tire looked...odd...within the frame, which itself is not a mirror image at the forward pivot.

I rummaged around for a straight edge and found a long piece of 1" steel square tubing. I laid that on top of the chain from the drive sprocket (it fit almost perfectly in a recess of the primary case) and then centered it as best I could on the chain back at the rear sprocket. This should establish a straight line of the chain. I next measured the gap between the metal tube and the rear wheel rim front and back and--surprise--found the gaps were dissimilar. I shifted everything again. With the rim gaps evened out and with complete disregard for the number of notches on the snail cams I was able to bolt the axle tight without anything moving. I can only surmise that the cams were not set properly to begin with. The rear wheel was probably in there cockeyed for who knew how long.

The chain was an absolute mess, covered in a thick coating of oil and phlegm of unknown origin. I took my parts cleaning solution and brush to it and scrubbed off the worst. The chain and sprockets were in good condition so I applied a light coat of clean oil. Everything spun happily and silently by hand. The slimy chain in concert with the missing chain guard had flung a black film over most everything on the left side of the bike. The underside of the rear fender was so bad I had to dunk it in my parts washer and scrub it clean. I assumed the PO had been a bit too enthusiastic with oiling the chain. Only later would I figure out that the crankcase pressure hose terminated just in front of the chain. An engine will build up pressure inside the lower end as it runs. The breather hose allows the pressure to be released safely but it also takes oil vapor with it. Royal Enfield cleverly utilized this wasted oily mist to keep the chain lubricated...at the expense of anything remaining clean for very long.

The Bullet engine has a total of three drain plugs. Unlike most motorcycles of the 1950s that had a separate tank to hold the engine oil Royal Enfield chose to incorporate the oil storage in the engine crankcase. This is how most vehicles of today are and it is just one example of how advanced some of the designs penned in Redditch, England were. I'd also read that Royal Enfield is credited with the first production use of a rear swinging suspension arm with twin shocks, a design that was ubiquitous until recent history when single shock systems took over. Anyway, I wanted to drain all the old fluids from the bike prior to starting the engine work. There was no oil showing on the dipstick nor did any drain out when I removed the main sump plug. There was still oil in the rear reservoir so I didn't concern myself with fearing it had run out of oil. Most likely the front sump was drained after the engine failure as part of the teardown. I removed the felt oil filter and checked it for metal and found none.

The bottom end of the engine would hopefully be fine.

By now I had received my digital edition of Pete Snidal's Bullet Service Manual. Despite the Bullet having been made for decades an English version of a shop manual was surprisingly difficult to come by. It didn't help that the Indian market and export models were frequently different in enough ways to make a 'factory' manual somewhat useless. Though Haynes makes one for the UCE Bullets they have never bothered to publish one for the iron barrel. Snidal, an enterprising Canadian who loved his Bullet, put together a collection of factory procedures, internet wisdom and personal experience and offered it to the world at large for a reasonable price. The 'Snidal Manual' is spoken of almost reverently in iron barrel circles.

In reading the manual the primary drive (big chain on the left side that drives the alternator and clutch) has it's own reservoir so I figured assessing the tension on the drive chain would be a good idea while checking the fluid level. I removed the inspection plug on the outer primary case and shone my light inside. Huh; didn't see anything. Stuck my finger in to test the chain tension which is supposed to be around a half inch free-play. Dear heavens, I could feel the chain flopping around with barely any tension on it. I figured there must be at least an inch and a half of play! Okay, I guess we're pulling off the primary cover which is actually easy.

Once inside I confirmed that the chain was

insanely loose. There is a threaded tensioner in the bottom of the case that pushes up on the drive chain to take out slack. Lifting up on the tensioner my chain impacted a boss on the inner housing before getting fully taught. In fact, the boss had visibly been ground off somewhat by the chain. It looked like a PO or some inept mechanic tried running the tensioner up the whole way. I imagined it made a hellish racket as the primary chain eroded the boss on the inner case.

Okay, so I couldn't use the tensioner to remove the slack without the chain grinding the case. I carefully examined the various gears and consulted my new manual but come away with no solution. The chain simply appeared to be too long. Additionally it looked nearly new, so coupled with the low miles on the odometer I seriously doubted the primary chain had stretched an entire inch since the bike was built. The condition of the chain and the near sterile condition of the primary case was, in fact, a bit suspicious.

My hypothesis was that the chain had been replaced with one the wrong size, possibly from a UCE Bullet. It wasn't far-fetched to believe that an unknowledgeable mechanic would order a primary chain for a Bullet not understanding there is more than one style. My 2007 was only a couple model years shy of the emergence of the unit construction engine which was completely different. I decided to order a primary chain and hoped it would solve the problem.

I'd amassed quite the list of parts for the sad

little Bullet by this time. The cylinder head was the most troubling. I endlessly debated several options. There was a used one on Ebay for $200 but I couldn't know the true condition of it. There was also a brand new one on Ebay from a USA seller for $325. A new one from Hitchcock's in England was $385 before shipping. I could also order a new one from India via Ebay for $240 which sounds like a bargain...except there were problems.

India is flush with parts and suppliers and the prices are often much lower. However, my careful research illustrated that the bargain price comes with several downsides. Shipping times from India are dreadful; there are often months of wait time for something to arrive...if it arrives at all. Reading feedback on various vendors it was all too common for parts to never appear, show up woefully late or arrive and be of such poor quality to be nearly useless. To be fair to the Indian people most all of the complaints included proper restitution of monies refunded when appropriate. It did not appear to be a theme of thievery, only poor service.

My tightwad nature simply couldn't be outdone by the desire to keep moving forward with repairing the Bullet. I'd heard good things about Hitchcocks in the UK and decided to give them a shot after finding a tested good used head available for the equivalent of $196. I order this along with a new standard size piston, rings and various gaskets. My credit card company refused the charges until I called them and confirmed that yes, I really had ordered several hundred dollars of motorcycle parts from some place in England.

Leakage

You may recall when I attempted to drain the old gas out of the fuel tank only the reserve side would drain. I removed the fuel petcock which has a brass screen as a filter. Most of it was clogged and the inside of the tank had a thin coating of rust. I'd half expected this. While I was working on the electrics and other things I had the tank sitting aside 'cooking'.

I engineered a plug for the outlet utilizing a couple hose clamps, a bolt and a short section of rubber hose. After a few times getting the clamps extra tight my contraption ceased dripping as I filled the tank with several gallons of white vinegar. There are various products you can use to attack rust in a fuel tank but mine appeared to be a fairly mild case. The vinegar is an inexpensive mild acid and not toxic which makes disposal easier.

I'd also dropped in about a dozen drywall screws to act as an abrasive when I would slosh the vinegar around the inside of the tank once or twice a day. The screws ultimately weren't terribly effective and I wouldn't recommend this method. I found them hard to extract later (be sure to count how many you drop in so you know you've removed them all). I later used a length of chain to do the scraping of the tank's innards and found it far more efficient.

As noted, vinegar is a mild acid. The longer it is allowed to do it's thing the better the results will be so I left it 'cooking' for a couple weeks with the tank perched atop a contractor's bucked in case my homespun plug failed. It would drip occasionally which added a nice vinegar odor to the garage. That is assuming one likes the smell of vinegar.

As I was working on the Enfield one day the vinegar scent seemed a bit more pronounced. Looking at the fuel tank I noticed there was a small puddle of vinegar on the floor outside the bucket. Odd. There were a few tiny beads on the outside of the tank that I wiped away with my finger. I mused that it must have dribbled out of the filler cap last time I sloshed it. I picked the tank up and shook it a bit, turning it this way and that and trying to get the drywall screws inside to do their thing. As I was holding it in a position with the front towards the ceiling I caught sight of a near microscopic stream of liquid pissing out of the part of the tank that would be closest to the seat. What the--?

I placed the tank back on the bucket and found the tiny beads of liquid again. I wiped them away. They reappeared. I looked closely at the tank and rubbed my fingernail over what looked like a small piece of dirt on the chrome.

It was a pinhole.

This was a major blow. My shoulders slumped. The Bullet Deluxe gas tank is chrome plated steel with the 'body' color and lettering painted on the sides and top. The painted part was bordered by tape pinstriping (a rant about that will follow shortly). With a typical painted, non-chrome fuel tank a pinhole is often a minor irritation. You simply weld it shut, grind and finish the metal and repaint the tank. Unfortunately with chrome you can't really do that as you ruin the plating in the process. The only way to fix it is to have the tank re-chromed--which is cost prohibitive--or replace it with another one. While Bullet fuel tanks aren't terribly expensive compared to other brands it was still a several hundred dollar proposition to replace. A used one would be terribly risky as mine looked perfectly fine on the outside. There was no easy way to tell something I'd be buying over the internet didn't have the same problems.

I knew from my car restoration background that there were products available to seal rusty old gas tanks but I had no idea if they could line one well enough to stop a pinhole leak. I began reading everything I could find on the internet about sealing tanks and the various products offered. The good news was that most of the products would seal up the type of hole I had with no trouble. The bad news was that there was an involved process to 'prep' the tank for the sealer and a lot of the products were on the expensive side, though still cheaper than a new tank.

I grumbled quietly to myself about this unwanted development. The engine parts had arrived and I knew it wouldn't take long to put it back together. In a few days' time I could have had it ready to attempt a start. Now, however, I had no fuel tank and it would take some time to get the sealer, prep the tank and apply the product. Most of the products required several days drying time as well. What progress I had been making would grind to a halt.

A brief interlude, if I may?

One of the things that had charmed me about the Royal Enfield were videos I had watched online of workers at the factory applying the pinstriping to the gas tanks. At the time there were two men doing this who I believe were brothers. They would stripe the tanks by hand, completely freestyle. It was a marvel to watch. They were quick about it too; I recently watched a tank being striped in a factory of a different brand and it took the worker as long to do one tank as the Enfield fellas needed to do two or three. The gold leaf striping was applied to black painted tanks in all of the videos I had watched and done in the exact same pattern as what was on my chrome Deluxe tank. Yet mine had cheap stick on striping. This has always been a note of disappointment with my bike and I someday hope to have a local professional stripe it by hand as nature and the ghosts of Redditch intended.

Back to the problem at hand. I drained the vinegar from the tank-with-the-vinyl-stripes and peered inside, expecting reasonably clean metal to greet me. Instead I saw the same tan/brown discoloration that was there before. As I fished out my ineffective drywall screws (most had merely wedged themselves in recesses) I noticed what looked like a crack in the bottom on one side. It wasn't in the metal; the crack appeared to be in something that looked like caulking. Did Royal Enfield use some sort of seam sealer along the weld lines? I prodded with a screwdriver and it did indeed feel like some sort of caulk. The more I looked at the inside of the tank with a telescoping light I came to realize the tank already had some sort of sealer in it--and it was failing. Fabulous.

With an array of screwdrivers and long needle nose pliers I began poking the sealer, getting it to come loose and pulling it out. Big, ugly chunks were removed while other stubborn pieces remained in place. I scraped, poked and chiseled, loosening up material and repeatedly blowing it out with pressure from an air gun. This was more effective than trying to shake it out past the lip of the filler neck but it had to be performed outdoors as old liner and rust scale went everywhere, including all over yours truly. It was an absolute mess.

I spent several evenings doing this, adding the length of chain to my repertoire of removal tools and shaking the tank violently to break loose pieces my other tools couldn't reach. If the outside of my tank hadn't looked so pristine I'd have given up and tossed it for a painfully expensive new one. For some reason I was determined to salvage this one. I felt a need to be victorious over this particular setback.

I finally got to a point where there was nothing more that I could do. There were still some pieces stuck to the inside, particularly around the fuel outlet where it had pooled. I'd concluded the sealer was probably a particular brand that had a poor reputation and had read that certain chemicals could be used to soften it to a liquid. One such product was acetone.

Acetone is nasty stuff. The vapors are dangerous to breathe and it can't safely be used without a proper respirator. I picked up a quart of the stuff at the local hardware store along with a respirator. This latter component irritated me as I had thought I still had one from my last car painting escapade but couldn't find it anywhere. So I purchased a brand new one, something I probably would never use again after this project. I donned rubber gloves, respirator and eye protection, took the tank outdoors where the fumes could dissipate and poured the toxic liquid into my tank. I had plugged the outlet again and put the fuel cap back on, then wrapped the entire tank in cling wrap in such a way that if anything should leak out it wouldn't damage the paint. I shook and sloshed as long as I could tolerate it, then drained the used product back into the can using a strainer. The acetone proved effective, though it would take several turns in the tank and even sitting for a period to finally melt all of the sealer away.

After endless research I'd settled on using a sealer called Red Kote. It was affordable, did not require mixing anything together and was not a multi-step process. I carefully read the instructions multiple times as online commentary made it clear that occasions where the product failed it was most often because the user had strayed from the directions. This was a new world to conquer and if it went wrong I'd have one giant mess on my hands.

The one tricky part was that the acetone rinse had to be neutralized by clean water. This was an easy thing to accomplish but the now clean and bare inside of the tank could quickly flash rust from the moisture. Yet the tank needed to be totally dry inside before applying the Red Kote. Fortunately it was a warm time of year so if the tank were left to dry after blowing the bulk of leftover moisture out with air I could be certain of no water fouling things up. The flash rust possibility still bothered me until I realized that whatever thin coating of rust may happen to develop would be covered completely by the sealer anyway. With that stress dismissed I prepared to pour in the red goop.

Once again I sealed the outlet, wrapped the tank in plastic cling wrap and had some wax paper at the ready to stick under the fuel cap (it is a locking cap and the sealer would gum up the catch otherwise). I'd also placed a piece of tape over the pinhole area to help seal it. I poured in the entire contents of the can then methodically spun the tank in various ways working to get a level coating of sealer on every surface. This was fairly nerve-wracking as you can't stop the incessant twirling or the sealer can pool and become too thick to ever fully dry. After the recommended period of time I removed the plug from the outlet and quickly drained the excess back into the can. The liquid soon began to get stringy which meant it was starting to solidify. I quickly replaced the plug and began twisting and turning once again. After another directed period of time I was able to open the cap and have a look inside. Everything was coated in candy apple red. I made sure it was firm enough not to flow anymore, then left it overnight in a position that wouldn't have it pool at the bottom...just in case.

For some reason I thought I'd read that the curing time was around forty-eight hours. The sealer would eventually 'flash-off' (all the solvents would evaporate out) and there would be no chemical odor. After three days I re-read the instructions only to confirm it would be cured when the smell dissipated; there was no actual calendar time for full curing.

Rats.

The pungent scent from the tank was remaining strong. What it needed was air flow but there was no way to efficiently attach a fan to it. Instead I got my compressed air blow gun out. With the compressor providing a constant air source I pulled the trigger just enough so that a light whisper of circulating air came out, then taped the trigger in that position. I stuck the nozzle inside the filler neck, repositioning it every half hour or so. I'd do this each evening for a few hours, not wanting to overtax my handyman size air compressor. After almost a week of circulating air through the tank the solvent smell was barely perceptible. I hoped it would be good enough as by now I had reached the point of being ready to fire the engine.

I'd also used the respirator during the coating process as the fumes were equally as worrisome as those from the acetone. When I was finished with the job I put the respirator into a drawer of one of my toolboxes...right next to the respirator I had been unable to find!

Putting A Ring
(Or Three)
On It

Let's back up a bit.

My package from Hitchcocks arrived four short days after I'd paid for the order. I was astounded and pleased by the fast service. The shipping fee was a bit painful but it was quickly forgotten by the clean and undamaged used head that shared the box with a new piston, ring set, gaskets and other bits and bobs. The piston in particular was very sexy; bright machined aluminum glistening in complete contrast to the carbon and oil stained mess that was still in my engine. Though I had not been planning to work on the Bullet that day the Hitchcocks order inspired me to get busy.

Routing and repairing wires and fixing chain tension were tasks I had been familiar with. Though I'd had my hands in the bowels of many a car or truck engine dismantling the Enfield's 500cc single would be uncharted waters. The first order of business was to remove the cast iron cylinder barrel so that I could access the piston.

The cylinder slides down over six studs and is held on by nuts. The nuts came off with no drama and I lightly tapped the cylinder upwards with a plastic mallet while being careful not to damage the cooling fins. The barrel came up and off the studs which allowed the piston and most of the connecting rod to protrude stoically from the crankcase. I'd stuffed some rags around the rod to keep debris from getting into the crankcase as well as to protect the rod from contacting the sides of the case.

One quirk of the cylinder barrel is it's interface with the engine casing. The bottom portion of the barrel casting slides down inside the crankcase. There is a 'stepped' joint where the two meet at the same level where the head gasket is placed. The barrel needs to contact the case leaving a proper size gap for the thickness of the head gasket. Debris left in this joint can prevent the cylinder from fully seating, which in turn fails to compress the head gasket properly and oil leaks will follow. I cleaned all of this, then test fitted the cylinder and measured the gap with feeler gauges around the circumference. The Snidal manual stressed the importance of getting it right as to fix it later would mean a significant teardown. To help assure an oil tight seal I added a light coating of gasket sealant around the oil passages on the gasket.

The piston is held to the connecting rod by a pin that slides through it. Recessed into the piston at each end are metal snap rings which are similar to 'C' clips but have small holes in them that allow easy removal with special pliers. These came out with no drama.

The piston pin is a snug fit and will not slide out on it's own. It required tapping it through with a drift and hammer while trying to keep the rod from being twisted against the crankshaft. Wedging the rod in place with pieces of wood proved effective and soon the mangled piston was free.

I measured the diameter of both old and new piston and was relieved to find they were the same size.

After sliding a ring into the cylinder and checking the bore/ring gap I installed the new rings on the piston in the proper order, alternating the location of the gaps. To ease the installation of the new piston I'd stuck the pin in the freezer hoping it would shrink ever-so-slightly making it slide in with little fuss. While it seemed to help I still needed to *cautiously* tap the pin through the piston and rod until it contacted the far side snap ring.

Now what?

The cylinder barrel now had to be lowered onto the engine case while feeding the new piston into it from the bottom. The procedure I was used to had me lower pistons and rods down from the top into a bore while using a ring compressor to get the expanding rings past the top opening. I couldn't do that with the Enfield as there was no way to access the rod bolts with the engine in the bike. Internet consultants assured it could be done by hand. It entailed using my fingers to compress one ring at a time while working the piston up into the bore. It sounded impossible and in the first several attempts I was certain it was. I was paranoid about accidentally breaking one of the somewhat fragile compression rings but to my eventual amazement the piston slid in past the first ring land. I repeated the process twice more despite the multi-piece oil ring doing it's best to thwart me.

Nearly a year later I would find a video online of a mechanic in India installing the barrel onto a Bullet with the piston already pushed into the bore just past the last ring. The barrel and piston were slid down over the studs and the rod and pin were then connected. The barrel was then pushed down onto the engine case; a far less fiddly way of accomplishing the same task.

At this point the engine was back to the same state of assembly it had been in when I purchased the bike. I still had a cylinder head and a box of assorted valve train parts and hardware to assemble. I'd mocked up the rocker arms, valve covers and all the hardware to figure out how it all went together. Fortunately most of the parts only fit one way and I was actually stunned that all the needed nuts and washers were rolling around in the box.

One task I wanted to perform was to lap in the valves on the replacement head. I had no idea how many miles were on the engine it came off of. By using a small amount of grinding compound between the valve and the seat I could make certain of a tight seal when they were closed. To perform this task the valves had to be loose, which meant the springs and retainers needed to come off. The box of parts had come with a small valve spring compressor tool but it would not work on the Bullet head. Ditto my large C-clamp style tool I use on just about everything. The head casting of the Bullet had a boss that was too close to the valve spring. Coupled with the near forty-five degree angle of the valves I did not have enough room to get the springs compressed far enough to remove the retainers.

I stared. I poked. I cursed appropriately. I couldn't come up with a solution to get the valve springs compressed. Though I'm no perfectionist I was loathe to install a head that I couldn't be certain had valves the would seal properly.

It finally occurred to me I could test the sealing of the valves. I turned the head with the combustion chamber facing up and poured water until it filled the 'bowl' of the chamber which completely covered the valves. If the valves were not sealing tightly against the seats I should find water seeping past them and dripping out the other side.

After several minutes everything remained dry. I ceased worrying about lapping valves.

The used replacement head needed very little cleaning but came with none of the studs that everything up top were held on by. This required removing all of the studs from the old damaged head and installing them in the new head. This worried me for two reasons: first, often studs like this will become overly attached to the casting they are in and refuse to come out. Second, Indian Royal Enfield metallurgy wasn't known for it's durability. The aluminum castings were often criticized as being too 'soft' making it very easy to strip out machined holes such as the ones all of these little studs threaded into. I began the process of removing them by installing a nut on the stud, then adding a second nut until they met, then tightening them firmly together. 'Double Nutting' allows you to use a wrench on the lower nut while the upper nut keeps it from turning. This transfers the force to the stud which will then (hopefully) unthread from the casting. Imagine my surprise and happiness when all of the studs came out without fuss and threaded into the replacement head with no trouble.

At this time I pulled the two pushrods out of the parts box to install them. They have adjusters threaded onto the bottom that are used to set the valve clearances. One of the adjusters looked like it was bent slightly. I set the pushrods on my workbench and on a whim rolled them across the surface. The one with the bent-looking adjuster rolled perfectly. The other one went woomp-woomp-woomp; I only now saw that it was obviously bent.

I cursed yet again. Another tremendous setback as I couldn't finish the head installation without them and it was not a part available anywhere nearby. I posted my tale of woe online and received a response from another Enfield enthusiast from across the country who said he thought he had some. After several days waiting for a reply and a few gentle prodding follow up emails later a response never materialized. I don't mind people not being able to follow through on something but what I can't abide is never responding and delaying me further. I called the individual an unpleasant name in the safety of my home on the other side of the country and set about placing another order with the fine folks at Hitchcocks...which was okay, as in the interim I'd managed to break something else.

Whoa, Part 1

In between doing all of these other jobs I would mix in fixing random annoyances for variety. One such thing was the front brake lever. The handle was excessively floppy (that word again) in the handlebar clamp. I took it apart and examined the pivot. The handle was aluminum and the pivot hole was oblong from wear. I took it to my local hardware store and poked through the aisle full of bins that held little springs, bushings and fasteners until I found a metal sleeve with the correct inside diameter. I drilled the lever out to accept the sleeve and trimmed the sleeve depth to fit inside the lever. Brilliant; it worked smoothly without flopping around. When I went to install it in the bracket on the handlebar it wouldn't quite go in. Oh yeah, I think I tried squeezing that piece together with pliers thinking that was the problem. I took a small pry bar and tried to spread the ears apart a bit.

Crack.

It was only at this point I saw that the

handlebar bracket was a cast piece and not stamped steel. Cast parts don't like to bend, something now illustrated clearly in front of me. There was no salvaging it. The only solution was to buy a new one which naturally came with a new lever. I had spent a couple of hours diagnosing it, running to the store for tiny parts and machining everything to fit. Up until the point of the *crack* I'd been pretty pleased with myself for repairing something instead of just tossing it for a new one. Now I contemplated the wisdom of all that time wasted for a part that only cost $34.97.

This was the point of the Bullet project though; I wanted to use my acquired tools and talent (such as it was) to give my hands and mind something to do.

Another little thing that bugged me was the front fender. I'd noticed a heavy rub mark on the left fork where the paint was completely gone. The Bullet has forks that slide up inside metal tubes; these protect the polished shock absorber of the fork from dirt and water. The fender moves up and down with the wheel and lower part of the forks. It is a pretty tight fit between the forks and my fender was offset to the left and had been rubbing against the fork cover for quite some time.

At first I thought the fender was twisted or the six metal 'legs' that hold the fender to the axle. Instead I found that one of the legs was cracked from fatigue. I pulled the fender and the legs off as a unit, then removed the broken leg pieces to see if anything could be done with it. Another chrome part made of not-very-thick steel. While it could be welded the results would be pretty ugly. I found a few on Ebay but they were all of the painted variety and not in keeping with the style of my Deluxe.

Off to the Hitchcocks catalog again and I found they sold replacements that were far stouter than the originals. It seemed only the middle ones were failure prone so I added one to my order. While getting a pair may have been wiser I actually had a morbid curiosity to see how long the other one might last.

I tapped out a dent in the bottom of the fender. It wasn't a highly visible spot and only I really know it's still a blemish. I lightly sanded the scraped up fork tube and sprayed the area with a satin black that hid the repair nicely.

I'd taken the front apart this far so elected to pull the front wheel off and have a look at the front brakes. Bullets are not known for having very good brakes but if everything is optimized and set up properly they were reported to at least be adequate. I pulled the brake drum off to examine the shoes and found them looking almost new. The arrangement is called a 'twin leading shoe' as there are two brake shoes inside the drum pretty much like you'd find on a car. Older motorcycles often had a 'single leading shoe' system which contained (oddly) two brake shoes that worked in a more bizarre and less effective fashion. On the Bullet each shoe was enacted by a sort of cam that rotated via a very complicated looking lever arrangement on the outside of the hub. I lightly greased the pivots being careful not to allow any excess to touch the actual lining and checked they worked freely before putting the hub back together. With the wheel installed once again I spun it by hand to make sure nothing was sticking. When I pulled the brake lever the wheel stopped. However, the pull required at the handlebar seemed long. The brake cable comes down vertically and attaches to the bottom lever on the hub. When the handle is pulled the cable tugs the lever up. The opposite end pivots down, pulling a rod with it that is threaded into the upper lever on the hub. All of this action moves the cams that apply the shoes inside the wheel hub that Jack built.

There are threaded adjustments for all of this nonsense and the ultimate goal is to have both brake shoes touch the inside of the brake drum at the same time for maximum effectiveness. I played around with it until it seemed improvement had been made, then set all the locking nuts. I'd ridden several other vintage bikes with drum brakes before so assumed the Bullet's would be at least adequate for it's weight and speed capability. No way to know for sure until it ran.

One of the parts that had arrived with the cylinder head was a new primary chain. This was the floppy chain found in the transmission side that didn't seem to fit and had ground away a chunk of the primary case. The chain went around a sprocket attached to the engine crankshaft then transferred the energy back to a sprocket behind the clutch which was attached by another shaft to the transmission. To replace the primary chain I'd have to remove the clutch, chain tensioner and alternator. This was another area of deep mystery to me but the Snidal manual made it sound like not a particularly big deal. It required some large sockets that I fortunately had, a torque wrench and a means of locking the whole mess from turning while the nuts were removed. The instructions suggested a piece of hardwood but all I had were various pieces of pine that were utterly useless. As soon as I tried to undo the alternator nut the wedge of wood simply splintered. After pondering over the roadblock for a day I finally dug through my box of what I call 'shapes' and found a leftover piece of stout aluminum angle. It fit perfectly within the gears I needed to lock and the soft aluminum did not mar the steel teeth. Brilliant!

With minimal difficulty I was able to remove the two parts of the alternator, the inner rotor and the outer stationary winding. Next the clutch came off as a myriad of discs and plates all kept in careful order. A few bolts to remove the tensioning device and it was out. With a bit of light prying, wiggling and help from a steering wheel puller the primary gears slid off their shafts and the assembly with the chain lay limp in my hands.

I wasted no time in putting the new chain on the gears and installing it all back inside the case. With the tensioner loosely installed the chain had virtually no slack. The other chain had clearly been the wrong one.

Time to put the clutch back on followed by the

alternator. The rotor gets installed first followed by the winding ring. There is a gap that must be maintained between the two parts around the entire circumference to 1) avoid the parts making contact and damaging them and 2) to allow for the system to charge properly. This is called an 'air gap'. Normally, setting such a gap is not terribly difficult but the rotor and ring are magnetically attracted. There are three bolts that attach the ring and when the gap is correct at one spot the magnetic pull will pull it too tight in another. Using two sets of feeler gauges I chased the gap around and around, fussing that it wasn't spot on and tapping it a bit one way or the other only to have it jump completely the wrong way. I think I spent nearly forty minutes working to get the air gap correct the whole way around.

I buttoned up the primary side by replacing the outer cover then filling the case with Type F automatic transmission fluid as had been recommended. The case held less than I expected but upon completion there were no leaks. The primary side appeared to be--as the Brits say-- properly sorted.

Which Way Is Up?

The Indian made Bullet comes with a Mikcarb carburetor which is a licensed copy of the Japanese Mikuni. You would think a duplicated Japanese carb would be reliable.

You'd be wrong.

Most Mikcarbs get quickly tossed in favor of other alternatives that offer better reliability and performance. Most owners will 'revert' to the classic British Amal carb but my Bullet came with a PKW which was an upgrade sold by the original importer. My carb was zip tied to the frame backbone and dangling free except for the throttle cable. The float bowl screws up from the bottom so removal of just the bowl for cleaning is easy. I found a small amount of white corrosion but no gunk or rust. It appeared the fuel had been drained or evaporated before it went into storage. I took out the float and needle valve and cleaned those as well. With everything cleansed I attempted to stick the bowl back on and I could not get it to go. There is a breather tube of some sort in the bowl that is on an angle that goes between the float and another casting on the upper carb body. With the floats out I can put it together easily. Floats in and no go. I must have spent an hour screwing with the thing and finally had to quit as I was starting to lose my patience. There must be a secret handshake to get it to go together but I haven't figured it out. I mean, it is just two parts that have to mate up for crying out loud!

I posted my frustration on one of the internet forums then set about installing a used chain guard that showed up that day. I'd found it on Ebay, a black painted one for a whole $17. While the Deluxe model came with a chrome one the low cost of the painted version was too good to pass up. Additionally, with the amount of grease and oil the chain seemed to fling around I wouldn't need to keep this one as spotless.

With that improvement made I worked on the clutch lever clamp on the handlebar which had a stripped hole. I re-tapped the threads to first oversize then pawed through my bins of hardware until I found the correct one. It was a bit long but a cutoff wheel made quick work of it. I also applied some stair tread traction tape in a loop around the handlebars which was the perfect solution to the weak clamping of the control housings. They no longer would 'walk' around the bars.

A day or so later I returned to the carburetor problem. I tried putting things together in multiple ways but nothing seemed to work. I just couldn't understand how it had come apart so easily but wouldn't pop back together. It had been suggested to me that I may have been putting the float in upside down. I had looked at it multiple times but it could only go together one way.

Except it didn't. When I finally submitted to the impossibility that it would go together the total opposite way of every other float I'd held in my hands the bowl slid together with the carb housing smoothly.

Facepalm.

Electrons, Part Two

The original turn signals/indicators were missing from my Bullet along with the original brake light and license plate bracket. I wasn't bothered by this as both were too modern and ugly to be on a machine so classically styled as the Bullet. The PO had purchased a Lucas replica brake light that came with a nice cast metal chrome housing. The turn signals that came in the box were not in great shape nor were they particularly attractive. I wound up buying four small Chinese chrome 'bullet' indicators off Ebay for a pittance. I considered them a temporary measure until I could find something I really liked but after hanging them on the bike had to admit they looked fine.

The bike did come with the brackets for the front indicators which attach behind the fork tubes. The original rear ones mounted to the big license bracket that I no longer had, so a new solution was needed. I was prepared to fabricate some simple metal tabs but wound up buying a pair of pre-made, black painted ones from China on Ebay that cost me only a couple of bucks...with free shipping! Whatever I could have made would not have looked as nice and would also have taken a good hour or more to make.

Insert boring and inflammatory discussion of China, trade policies, American jobs, tariffs and unions here. Done; now we can move on.

Meanwhile, I began sorting out the wiring for the indicators. The connectors for the rear ones had been hacked off. The front ones...well, I'll be damned if I could find them! There were two unused leads inside the headlamp nacelle but during circuit testing had no power going to them. Instead, the Bullet has two small lamps above the headlamp called 'trafficators' that blinked--with marginal enthusiasm--when the switch was thrown.

Oh...the flasher. Royal Enfield uses an odd rectangular flasher to blink the lights on and off. Mine did nothing. I pulled the one from my older Ford pickup and plugged it in and things began blinking. Tried the Enfield one; nothing. Found a 'spare' automotive flasher in my cupboard and it also worked. I left it dangling inside the right tool box as I continued my efforts.

I wound up with the left signals flashing slowly like some sort of geriatric lighthouse beacon. The right indicators did nothing while the brake light blinked in a proper rhythm and the AMP meter pegged to the discharge side.

Something was amiss. I went through the

connections, took off my Chinese brackets and signal lamps and removed whatever paint or coating may have been causing havoc with the grounds. Put it all back together with the exact same result.

The turn signal switch got taken apart next; you can actually disassemble it. I cleaned the contacts that didn't appear dirty and put it back together, a task that can best be defined as 'fiddly'. Still no change.

One thing I had not checked was the bulbs in the trafficators. I swapped them left to right and things changed. After examining the bulbs and finding them to be dissimilar wattage I rummaged through my bin of bulbs until I found another match. With two bulbs of the same output things blinked as they were supposed to. The flasher requires a certain current draw to operate which is why when people often install LED lights they will flash rapidly. The one incorrect bulb was actually causing the opposite effect.

All was fine...until it stopped working again and the brake light began flashing. Something was crossed up somewhere for that to happen and I assumed it had to be some of the new wiring I had made to extend the snipped off indicator connectors. As I played around with checking the grounds for the umpteenth time I saw a spark from inside the fender. I jiggled the harness that clips to the underside of the fender until it sparked again and discovered a spot where the original harness was worn through as if it had dropped down onto the rear tire at some point. Though I had to pull the rear fender off to repair it the fix was simple. It made me feel good knowing the problem wasn't something I'd caused. Finally, all the electrons were flowing to the proper places.

The Moment Of Truth

At last, the pushrods arrived.

Each one is a different length and I had to
consult the Hitchcocks catalog to know which
went where. I slid them in place, bottomed out the
adjusters then attached the rocker arms to the
cylinder head. Next came the setting of the valve
lash. The pushrods have threaded adjustments at
the bottom that set the clearance between
themselves and the rocker arms. I'd read much
about Royal Enfield valve adjustment and that it
was something that needed to be checked with
frequency. A running joke of Royal Enfield
owners was the adage 'Loud Valves Save Lives'.
The Snidal manual dismissed with using any type
of measuring device and instead offered this
simple guideline: the pushrod adjustment should
be set where it makes contact with the rocker arm
tight enough that the pushrod won't rattle but can
still be turned by finger effort.

I found this both amusing and somewhat
dubious. Never in all my years of working on

engines had there not been a very specific mathematical clearance involved. But I did as instructed, running the adjusters up until they just touched the rocker arm, checking that the pushrod could still be 'spun' with light pressure then tightening the lock nut. Simply ludicrous.

The rocker covers went on last with their arrangement of specific length bolts that threaded down over the studs in the cylinder head. The very last one of these I tightened to the torque specification in the manual stripped out. I couldn't believe it! I'd been so careful with all of the fasteners and never exceeded the recommendations in the manual. Fortunately it was just a rocker cover and the part seemed to be held on well enough by the remaining bolts. I added a small bit of thread locker to the final bolt, hand tightened it until it was snug and left it to dry.

When I mentioned this to some Enfield owners later they all shook their heads and 'tsk-tsk'd' me, advising that the torque specs in the manual should be ignored. "Just make them nice and tight," the one fellow told me. "Those values may have worked on the British models but you're lucky you didn't pull more studs on yours using those." Lesson learned.

The Bullet has a decompressor which is a third, small valve in the head activated by a cable that runs to the left handlebar. When the cable is pulled the valve will open, releasing the pressure in the cylinder on the compression stroke to make starting easier. It is also a good idea to use on a

Bullet for shutting the engine down as it helps avoid 'kickback' which can damage the engine. Getting the compression release valve together and installed was a tricky process and when I was finished I found it wouldn't work. After numerous internet forum discussions and sharing photos and even a video of my particular Bullet no one could figure out why mine wouldn't work. It was as if the cable was too long; yet I bought a replacement and it was the exact same length with identical fittings. After fussing with it for several days I finally threw my hands up and decided I didn't need the cable. Instead I would just reach down with my hand and push the spring loaded valve open until the engine stopped. I always wore gloves when I rode so wasn't too concerned about burning myself.

With the engine finished I installed the fuel tank and the new seat. I'd stressed over the seat situation for quite awhile as I didn't care for the original (missing from mine, remember) two person seat. I just didn't think it looked right for such an antique looking motorcycle. My wife never rides pillion so I didn't need seating capacity for a passenger and felt a solo seat would look appropriate. I liked the solo seats on the newer UCE Classic models but they were not interchangeable. Hitchcocks offered several options and I wound up buying a 'trials' seat from their 'blemishes and closeouts' section. The seat I purchased had a nearly invisible flaw in the leather that looked like a scratch. The Bullet was never going to be a showpiece and the savings made the price affordable enough for me to stomach the hit to my credit card. After I got it bolted to the bike I couldn't have been more pleased with the decision.

There were still two parts missing: the muffler and some sort of air cleaner. The rusty header pipe on mine was a discontinued version. I'd found another on Ebay but the seller wanted a pretty hefty price for a used exhaust part and I couldn't justify the cost for a machine that still hadn't run. Figuring I'd likely trash the system for something else later I opted for a cheap universal aftermarket muffler referred to as a 'cocktail shaker'. It looked appropriately vintage and slid over the existing pipe perfectly. However, the bracket to hold up the rear portion would not line up with anything on the Bullet. I would eventually have to fabricate something but it would be a complex piece with multiple bends. Screw it; I just tightened down the forward clamp as tight as I could make it and hoped the thing wouldn't fall off on the maiden voyage.

The last piece was the air filter. In my mind the perfect style was a chrome 'pancake' filter used on any number of British bikes in the 1950s and 1960s. And they were plentiful...but there was a problem. These filters were meant to fit Amal carburetors which had threaded inlets the filter base could screw onto. My PKW inlet had not threads and took a style of filter that slipped over the mouth and was held on by a simple clamp. There were a lot of filters that would fit but they were all cone shaped 'pod' filters that would like fine on a modern sports bike but ridiculous on a faux antique like the Bullet. Eventually I found one filter that would work from an Ebay vendor in (surprise) China. Though it took several weeks to arrive it fit perfectly and does a reasonable job of providing the look I was after. The filter would not arrive for some time until after my attempt to start the bike, however.

The day was finally here; the oil had been filled, fuel added, spark plug and point gap checked. There was nothing left to do. Would it start? Would the bottom end have a horrible death rattle? Would the transmission have all of the gears? Would a fuel line pop off and set it on fire? All of these apocalyptic thoughts crossed my mind as I wheeled the Bullet outside and perched it on the center stand. I set up my camera phone in case by some miracle the thing actually fired I would catch the moment.

I held the compression release valve open and kicked it over slowly about six times to make certain everything was free and to try to move some oil around in the engine since I had drained it completely. Fuel turned on. Ignition key turned on. Compression release closed. Kick engine slowly around until it locks. Release compression and kick slightly until the AMP needle kicks to the center. Check and recheck all my switches...and then, a healthy kick downward.

Nothing.

Go through the whole kick through--stop--decompressor--needle sequence again, then another kick.

Nothing.

Once more. Another hefty kick.

PuppPuppBrrrrraaaaaHHHHHH!

It's running! In fact it's running a bit too much and idling at probably two thousand rpm's...but it's running! No bottom end noise either.

I flicked the kill switch because of the high idle speed but found it did nothing so turned it off with the key.

I poked around a bit wondering if something on the carb was set incorrectly. Though possible it seemed unlikely. The bike had obviously run before with it set up as I'd found it. I twisted the throttle and released it but discerned nothing. I went through the starting procedure again and it fired right off. I turned the mixture screw on the carb back and forth but it didn't change anything. When I twisted the throttle the revs went up and stayed there even higher than before. I shut it off again. Something was amiss.

I pushed it back inside the garage and poked and jiggled the throttle cable. I'd used zip ties to hold the cables and wiring harness up against the backbone of the frame and wondered if I had pulled them too tight. It looked as if the carb slide was not fully closing. I had to remove the fuel tank to check and after it was off I twisted the throttle and found that the carb slide was now fully closed. The throttle cable had been pinched not by my zip ties but by the fuel tank when it was bolted down over everything. I rerouted the cable and refitted the tank. Twisted and released the throttle several times and the slide snapped fully closed each time. Problem solved!

This is when I notice the heavy drips of red transmission fluid falling from the primary case.

Royal Oilfield

My first thought was the primary cover seal was leaking. The cover itself is a large, one piece casting held on by a single large nut. The joint between the cover and casing is a giant rubber O-ring seal. Though I had purchased a new one the internet experts advised me that they could be re-used, so I had. After wiping off the excess it didn't appear it was the source. The fluid was either coming from the back of the case where it butted against the engine or from the case itself where there was either a casting line (I hoped) or a crack (I hoped not). Either way the case would need to come off which meant undoing all of the clutch, alternator and drive chain sprockets I had just put together. Sigh. I reminded myself that at least the engine ran.

So, off with the cover, shift lever, clutch, and alternator followed by the chain and the sprockets including the sprag clutch and gears for the starter. Holding the sprag clutch in my hand I could see how fragile it was and decided it wouldn't be going back in. Kick start only from here on! The primary case was now bare and only a few bolts held it to the engine. I removed those and tried pulling it off to no avail. A few stout whacks with my plastic hammer broke it free and I removed it. I got the thing apart and didn't see a crack (Whew!). What I also didn't see was *half the gasket for the inner cover.* There was *some* there but none where the leak was occurring. Another PO/bad mechanic signature fail!

It all started to add up in my Inspector Clouseau mind. The starter sprag clutch had probably been damaged. The dimwitted mechanic/PO pulled it apart to replace the sprag and clean out all the debris. At the time the primary chain was replaced with the wrong one. The would-be repairer hadn't ordered a gasket so just stuck the torn one back on and hoped for the best. While it had run I'm sure it made a lot of noise and most of the primary drive fluid had leaked out. It explained the nearly antiseptic cleanliness of the primary case when I first popped it open. I also wondered if the damage hadn't all been caused by the dropped valve. Perhaps the PO had repaired the primary side (incorrectly) and only then discovered the broken valve?

I also did not have a primary case gasket but I did have some good quality gasket-in-a-tube that would suffice. I cleaned the surfaces thoroughly, applied a sufficient but not excessive bead of sealant to the flange and carefully put the case back on, followed once again by all of the whirling and spinning parts that resided within the case proper. When I got to the alternator, however, I chose a different tactic than my multiple feeler gauges.

Thanks to a helpful suggestion I'd picked up on the internet I grabbed one of the empty gallon vinegar containers from the fuel tank project and cut it apart. The top supplied a handy funnel for use later. The bottom I further dissected until I had a circular piece of plastic with no top or bottom. I cut this yet again so that the plastic could be laid flat. I measured the circumference of the rotor then trimmed my plastic back so that when wrapped around the rotor the two ends met with little gap. With the rotor on and the plastic 'sleeve' around it I slid the winding collar over everything. The vinegar bottle thickness was close enough to the air gap measurement that all I needed to do was tighten the collar down. What had taken me forty minutes before now had only taken five.

I saved the plastic 'tool' and wrote on it in Sharpie "Royal Enfield alternator air gap tool" and stuck it on the shelf.

With the cover back on I filled the case with Type F again, watched for leaks and found none. What appeared to have been a crack had indeed just been a mold line from when the piece was cast. I pushed the Bullet outside and set about the starting routine. It was time to see if it would actually move under it's own power.

A post I made to an internet forum of motorcycle friends that had been following my resurrection of the Bullet is repeated here:

"Rode it double digit miles. Didn't die. More later."

Maiden Voyage

I'm sure you are dying to know what it is like to ride a Royal Enfield Bullet. Well, wonder no more my brethren, for I have ambled into the depths of Enfield piloting, survived, and will now share with you all you need to know.

First, if it isn't vibrating like a paint shaker it isn't running. You know how most motorcycles go 'thunk' into gear? The Bullet doesn't. It just sort of 'ticks' into first. Pull out with a little or a lot of throttle; either way the bike doesn't care. The machine will 'advance' at a pace it deems respectable. Shift up with authority. Shift down with a feather touch because if you don't the shifter moves into Gear Purgatory. This is sort of like a false neutral but a much more vast expanse of nothingness that would perplex even Carl Sagan. The brakes suck. I don't mean suck in a "Gee, I wish these were Brembos" way. They suck in a "Gee, I wish this thing actually had brakes" way. If you really squeeze the lever--with your whole hand, because using only two fingers does absolutely nothing--you feel the brakes apply. The bike won't slow any; you can just detect the brake shoes making contact with the drums.

So remember that Gear Purgatory I spoke of? Engine braking does most of the slowing on a Bullet. If you downshift into Gear Purgatory while trying to slow down with what they laughably call brakes on this contraption you'd best have your need for stopping somewhere far on the distant horizon. Your sphincter will clench and your penis will shrink "like a frightened turtle" as you pray to His Noodly Goodness that your forward momentum will decrease enough that you won't die when you hit whatever it is you are trying to slow down for.

On my particular Bullet the two foot pegs are positioned at two different heights because the cast brackets are bent. How I did not notice this before I can't explain. Also, the kick starter is cleverly positioned where your right heel should be, which isn't convenient or comfortable. And of course my turn signals don't work. Again. Which is super cool when I'm trying to slow for a turn, downshift in such a way I actually engage a lower gear and am signaling my intentions to the people behind me who are no doubt pissed as hell they got stuck behind a WAY TOO LOUD old India built motorcycle that struggles to get to 50 mph up any kind of slight rise in the geography.

So yeah, the Bullet is a complete success!

I had to put gas in it so went to a station nearby. The number of people who asked about the bike in the time it took me to pump two gallons: two.

"What year is that?"
"Did you restore it yourself?"
After riding it home and parking it in the garage I noticed red drips of Type F fluid on the floor under the bike...from a totally different location.

Repairing Repairs

After a few more test rides I had a list of things that needed attention. The Type F fluid leak was interesting in that it only puked while it was being ridden. Once I cleaned it up after a ride no more drips hit the floor. I quickly traced this to a shifter shaft seal on the back side of the primary case. A small rubber seal about the size of a nickel that would entail removing the inner case--again--and removing all of the gears, clutches, and chain--again.

Such was my joy that I chose to ignore that particular problem for the time being.

The other pressing issue was the brakes; in particular the front brake which seemed to be doing almost nothing to help slow the Bullet down. I'd ridden a number of old motorcycles from the sixties and seventies and none had exhibited braking as terrible as the Enfield. Though the bikes had a reputation for weak brakes there was no way I could believe mine were functioning properly.

While trying to adjust the hand lever for the front brake I thought something wasn't right at the wheel hub. After much head scratching and turning threaded adjustment components I came to the conclusion only half the front brake was being activated. There is a 'trunion' which is a ferrule looking thing that a threaded adjustment rod passes through that helps activate the brakes but also make them return. It was not just stripped but totally hogged out. I later found out this was a 'modification' to allow easier adjustment of the brakes. While it accomplishes that it doesn't provide the pull backwards to return the shoes to rest. The upper lever that activates the shoes at the top of the drum also looked to be indexed totally wrong. The top and bottom levers should have been parallel but weren't.

I spent several evenings trying to adjust the levers, threaded sleeves and cable to no avail. When I could get a good application of the shoes to the drum they would then 'stick' and drag inside the brake drum. I would have to either manually pull back on the bottom lever of the assembly or give the tire a good swift kick to release it, neither solution of which was obviously satisfactory. I'd obtained well-written instructions on how to properly adjust everything but the upper lever simply wouldn't return on it's own. I finally surmised that the 'modification' (actually recommended in one publication) was the culprit. The hogged out part was essentially a threaded adjuster someone had drilled to be a sleeve. The simple solution would be just to buy one but it was the first part I encountered that was no longer available. After staring at it for some time I saw what it needed: a collar to fill the gap between the butchered adjuster and the lever. I actually found a piece of brass tubing that was the correct diameter in my drawer of leftover bits (it pays to never throw any piece of scrap away!) and with it installed I was astounded to find that my bodge to repair a bodge worked like a charm. On the next test ride the brakes...well, let's just say they were massively improved. They were now capable of stopping the bike from speed. Once. I found it didn't take much to get them hot. Still, it was nice not having to rely on downshifting exclusively nor attempt to figure out how to carry an easily deployed anchor.

Another air mail order from Hitchcocks and a new shift shaft seal (say that fast three times) arrived. By now you likely have memorized the sequence to take it apart and put it back together; rest assured I am equally an expert. The old seal was rock hard and I suspect pulling it on and off the previous time was enough to tip the orbit of the moon slightly and cause it to leak. After reassembly the primary side remained bone dry. For awhile. It did start to weep again but at a level that is just an annoyance instead of a rapid dispensing system.

The final task I performed was to replace the muffler. The cheap straight-through version I'd clamped on was far too loud and would crackle and pop on deceleration like some sort of race bike, something the Bullet could never be confused with. After much hand-wringing and indecision I bought a supposedly blemished 'pea shooter' from Hitchcocks that I could find nothing wrong with. It also came with a hanger that looked correct but was at least an inch short. I fabbed one up out of a piece of flat steel, carefully replicating the bends on the supplied one but adding a few inches of length. With my homemade bracket the muffler looks nice, sounds sporty but not obnoxious and came with the added bonus of giving the bike more power. With the loud muffler attached the bike would struggle to ever get into fifth gear and any small rise would thwart it's speed. The replacement muffler apparently generated the correct amount of back pressure which increased torque. I found myself shifting into fifth gear more frequently. The Bullet seemed to have found it's stride and I made the comment to my wife that it was a 'happy' motorcycle.

Emma

I have three motorcycles: a 2008 Triumph Bonneville, a 2012 Triumph Tiger 800 and the Bullet. Each has a purpose. The Bonneville is my bike for cruising the two lane roads for an afternoon or entire day. The Tiger is for longer trips when I need to cover distance or want to explore some unpaved roads. The Bullet was purchased to be an educational experience and perhaps a sort of mechanical sculpture to display in our house. I was never convinced that I would care much for riding it after it was repaired. The specifications and performance statistics had never painted a promising picture.

The little Enfield has squirmed it's way into being an answer to something I didn't know was missing. The Bullet is the perfect motorcycle for short jaunts. I frequently will take it out for thirty minutes to an hour after work just motoring sedately around the less traveled (and relatively level) roads near my home. Though I have ridden it longer and farther I find it's duration of comfort hovers at around an hour. More than that and I start to tire of the seat, the foot pegs (still bent), the vibration through the handlebars and the mental alertness necessary to plan for stops and climbing hills. It is a very interactive machine from the time I start it until I push the decompressor and snick the key off.

The properly adjusted brakes are barely adequate. The engine weeps a bit of oil as does the primary case. The headlamp has illumination equivalent to a candle. You can sometimes feel the frame flex. The front fork seals may be starting to leak. The speedometer is so absurdly optimistic it makes you laugh. The tires are likely the original ones and should probably be replaced. The clutch slips until the fluid is warm. It has no side stand, fuel gauge or trip odometer and the bar end mirror it came with vibrates out of adjustment within a few hundred yards. By today's standards it is an awful motorcycle.

Despite all of the preceding complaints I can't imagine parting with it. When I take it out for a quick spin after work it immediately puts me in a good mood. It is easy to start. It is light, nimble and easy to push around. The fuel tank is surprisingly big and gas consumption is frugal. The clutch pull is light and the five speed transmission is clockwork smooth once you learn how to avoid Gear Purgatory. It is happier being revved out than lugged around at low RPMs. It makes cool sounds. Everyone loves it and thinks it is far older than it's 2007 build date. People often ask me what year it is and I simply answer,

"Guess". It makes for interesting conversations.

I broke a cardinal rule with this machine. I gave it a name. I don't anthropomorphize mechanical devices but for some reason I felt compelled to call it something other than 'the Bullet' or 'the Enfield'.

I named her Emma. No particular reason; the name just came to me and I thought it fit.

My original plan had been to buy a dilapidated motorcycle and rebuild it over the winter months. Emma had come to me in the early spring and like a child with a new toy I couldn't resist diving into repairing her. Most days the weather was pleasant and the garage door was open. Cool breezes wafted through the shop as I sat on my upturned bucket, listening to Samantha Fish singing on Alexa as I checked wiring or took the primary case apart for the umpteenth time. I'd grown up teaching myself mechanics by working on old cars and trucks. The years passed and the vehicles became more complex and the engine bays more compact. I'd been slowly losing interest in working on vehicles but hadn't realized it nor the reasons why. The modern machinery was more work than pleasure. Putting Emma back together was so organically simple and pleasurable the time just flew by. It never really felt like I was working on her, more like I was spending time doing something fun. When had I last just had *fun* using my tools? I viewed the other occupants of my garage with a fresh perspective and realized much of it wasn't where my heart truly was. The cars had gotten faster and the trucks more luxurious but something had been missing. I had unknowingly longed for the simplicity of a pure, honest machine to tinker with and the neglected Royal Enfield Bullet had been the answer.

The days shortened and my after-work rides began to cast longer shadows. As I rode along an empty two lane road I watched my silhouette float across the field next to me. If not for the outline of my full face helmet the profile I saw could easily have been of a younger man motoring along a narrow English lane astride his 1955 motorcycle...possibly headed to meet a pretty lass, backed by a soundtrack of a machine whose parts were working in pleasant harmony.

A happy motorcycle with her happy rider.

Epilogue

I paid $1200 for Emma in her disassembled state. After tallying up my receipts I had spent an additional $1155 on parts and materials to get her running and moving. $2255 total investment which is about what I could get for her in a private sale.

"But you could just have bought a running example for that," some would argue. Yes, I certainly could have. If you are a motorcyclist then you know the journey is more important than the destination. Why ride a motorcycle when you could just drive a car? The process of getting Emma into working condition was the journey; getting to ride her was the destination. I spent $2255 and I got not just a useful conveyance but an education. I can now tackle a lot of motorcycle repairs with a confidence that I didn't have before. I spent many enjoyable evenings and weekends doing something tactile and rewarding. I provided numerous followers on the internet with humorous stories and endless questions. And perhaps I've also inspired some of you to take on something equally as rewarding.

As I write this Emma is only a few feet away. She resides in my finished basement alongside my Bonneville. I made little platforms covered with leftover linoleum flooring to protect the carpet from the inevitable oil drops (from Emma; not the Triumph). It is nice having them indoors like this over the winter months. I steal a glance now and then and dream of warmer days and the satisfying sound of her engine firing off from a single kick. While we're waiting for better weather I browse motorcycles on Craigslist and Facebook Marketplace. Maybe a sad, broken, disassembled, unwanted Norton Commando will need rescuing.

Sources

https://accessories.hitchcocksmotorcycles.com/
At some point in the book you may get the idea I'm a shill for Hitchcocks but I assure you I am nothing but a satisfied customer. If you own a pre-UCE Bullet in the USA there is no dealer support. While there are a couple of small vendors or the risky India option you are far better clicking on the link above. Hitchcocks web site is well designed and easy to navigate. There is very little they don't have in stock and they even offer used parts. The staff were very helpful and quick to respond. Prices are quite reasonable and only the shipping cost from the UK to America is pricey. I can't say enough good things about the company and am grateful they exist.

http://www.enfield.20m.com/bullet1.htm
Pete Snidal's manual is a must-have before digging into a Bullet. It is available in digital form sent by email. Snidal doesn't do this as a business; it is more of a private endeavor. After sending

payment it took several days to receive the email with the download instructions. Be patient; Snidal does come through and you'll be glad you waited. The manual contains illustrations, instructions and a bit of Snidal humor. Remember, the available Haynes manual is only for the UCE models.

https://www.royalenfields.com/

David Blasco writes a weekly blog about Royal Enfield ownership in the US. His short but informative posts cover all sorts of topics. The blog has individual pages for tech tips, history and many other items of interest. He also aggregates various Enfields for sale from Craigslist, Ebay and other sources.

https://forum.classicmotorworks.com/

Though there are several message boards on the internet for Royal Enfield this one is based in the USA. Originally started by the old importer, Classic Motorworks, it has been taken over by Hitchcocks. There is a massive amount of good information stored here and I've received a great deal of good advice from some of the participants.

http://damonq.com/red-kote.html

Red Kote is the sealer I used for Emma's fuel tank. While it is not the only product available I found it one of the easier to use and least expensive. My experience with it (thus far!) has been very positive.

About The Author

David Wittlinger resides in central Pennsylvania with his wife Lynn and a rotating pack of rescued herding dogs. Since he began driving in 1982 he has owned over sixty vehicles though not all have been as successful as Emma. His previous works include three fiction novels: *The Strong One, Brianna's Reprisal* and *Portal To Elysium*. A short digital-only book *The Mid-Life Epiphany* was his first non-fiction book. He also authors the blog *Motorosophy* which examines the emotional attachments between people and their machines. His YouTube channel *Mongrel Motorsports* has additional videos on Emma the Royal Enfield and some of his other vehicles.

Printed in Great Britain
by Amazon

49614373R00057